# ICH GEHE GERN IN DIE KITA

# I LOVE TO GO TO DAYCARE

## Shelley Admont

Illustriert von Sonal Goyal und Sumit Sakhuja

First edition, 2016

Translated from English by Tess Parthum
Aus dem Englischen übersetzt von Tess Parthum

**I love to Go to Daycare (German English Bilingual Edition)/ Shelley Admont**

ISBN: 978-1-77268-332-5 paperback

ISBN: 978-1-77268-632-6 hardcover

ISBN: 978-1-77268-331-8 ebook

für die, die ich am meisten liebe-S.A.

for those I love the most-S.A.

*Jimmy lag in seinem Bett und umarmte seinen Lieblings-Teddybären. Er versuchte zu schlafen, aber etwas quälte ihn und hielt ihn wach.*

Jimmy was lying in his bed hugging his favorite teddy bear. He was really trying to sleep, but something bothered him and kept him wide awake.

*Er rollte aus dem Bett und ging auf die Suche nach seinen Eltern.*

He rolled out of bed and went to look for his parents.

*Unten im Wohnzimmer sahen seine Mama und sein Papa gerade fern. Mit seinem Teddy im Arm setzte sich Jimmy auf Mamas Schoß. „Mami, ich kann nicht schlafen", sagte er.*

Down in the living room, his mom and dad were watching TV.  Holding his teddy, Jimmy sat on Mom's lap. "Mommy, I can't sleep," he said.

*Mama zerzauste sein Haar und gab ihm einen Kuss. „Woran denkst du?"*

Mom ruffled his hair and gave him a kiss. "What are you thinking about?"

*„Ich denke an die Kita", flüsterte er und drückte Mama fest.*

"I'm thinking about daycare," he whispered and hugged Mom tightly.

*„Oh Schatz, die Kita macht so viel Spaß!", sagte Mama.*

"Oh, sweetie, daycare is so fun!" said Mom.

*„Du wirst dort neue Freunde kennenlernen", fügte Papa hinzu. „Es macht sogar so viel Spaß, dass ich mir wünsche, ich könnte auch mitgehen!"*

"You'll meet new friends there," added Dad. "In fact, it's so much fun that I wish I could go, too!"

*„Kann ich mit dir zuhause bleiben?", fragte Jimmy. Sein Kopf fiel auf Mamas Schulter.*

"Can I stay at home with you?" asked Jimmy. His head fell on Mom's shoulder.

*Mama streichelte seinen Kopf und schaute tief in seine Augen.*

Mom stroked his head, looking deeply into his eyes.

*„Wie wäre es damit", sagte sie. „Weil es dein erster Tag in der Kita ist, wirst du nur für zwei Stunden dort bleiben. Danach komme ich wieder, um dich nach Hause zu bringen. Aber ich bin mir sicher, dass du so viel Spaß haben wirst, dass du gar nicht gehen wollen wirst."*

"How about this," she said. "Since it's your first day in daycare, you'll only stay there for two hours. After that, I'll come back to take you home. But I'm sure that you'll have so much fun that you won't even want to leave."

„Weißt du was?", sagte Papa. „Du kannst sogar deinen Teddybären mitnehmen. Hört sich das gut an?" Jimmy nickte.

"You know what?" said Dad. "You can even take your teddy bear with you. Does that sound good?" Jimmy nodded.

*„Oh, du bist so ein großer und schlauer Junge",
murmelte Mama und küsste seine Stirn. „Ich bin
sicher, du bist müde. Lass uns ins Bett gehen."*

"Oh, you're such a big and smart boy," said Mom,
kissing his forehead. "I'm sure you're tired. Let's
go to bed."

*Sie brachte Jimmy in sein Zimmer und deckte ihn
zu. Dann gab sie ihm einen Gute-Nacht-Kuss und
flüsterte in sein Ohr: „Ich habe dich lieb, Schatz."*

She led Jimmy to his room and tucked him in.
Then, she gave him a goodnight kiss and
whispered in his ear, "I love you, sweetie."

*„Ich habe dich auch lieb, Mama", sagte Jimmy. Mit
einem großen Gähnen umarmte er seinen
Teddybären und schloss seine Augen.*

"I love you too, Mom," said Jimmy. With a big
yawn, he hugged his teddy bear and closed his
eyes.

*Jimmy war schon fast eingeschlafen, als er eine fremde Stimme hörte. „Hey, Jimmy!"*

Jimmy was almost asleep when he heard a strange voice. "Hey, Jimmy!"

*Er öffnete seine Augen und schaute umher. „Wer spricht da?", murmelte Jimmy.*

He opened his eyes, looking around. "Who's talking?" murmured Jimmy.

*„Ich bin es, dein Teddybär!"*

"It's me, your teddy bear!"

*Erstaunt schaute Jimmy nach unten. Der Teddybär winkte und lächelte. „Ich habe gesehen, dass du aufgewacht warst", sagte der Teddybär.*

Astonished, Jimmy looked down. The teddy bear waved his hand and smiled. "I saw you were upset," said the teddy bear.

*Jimmy seufzte tief. „Ja, ich gehe morgen in die Kita", murmelte er.*

Jimmy sighed deeply. "Yes, I'm going to daycare tomorrow," he mumbled.

*„Jimmy, mein Freund, aber ich gehe doch mit dir!" Der Teddybär zwinkerte ihm zu und schenkte ihm sein großes Teddybären-Lächeln.*

"Jimmy, my friend, but I'm going with you!" The teddy bear winked at Jimmy and gave him his big teddy-bear smile.

*Jimmy schaute ihm zu, springend und klatschend und brach in Gelächter aus.*
Jimmy looked at him jumping and clapping and burst out laughing.

*„Pssst", flüsterte der Teddybär. Er zeigte auf Jimmys zwei ältere Brüder, die in ihren Betten schliefen.*

"Shhhh," whispered the teddy bear. He pointed to Jimmy's two older brothers, who were sleeping in their beds.

Er sprang in Jimmys Arme und kuschelte sich fest an ihn. „Gute Nacht, mein Freund!"

He jumped into Jimmy's arms and cuddled him close. "Goodnight, my friend!"

*Am nächsten Morgen sprangen seine beiden älteren Brüder aus dem Bett und gingen zu Jimmy.*

The next morning his two older brothers jumped out of bed and walked over to Jimmy.

*„Heute ist dein erster Tag in der Kita. Du hast so ein Glück", sagte sein ältester Bruder.*

"Today is your first day in daycare. You are so lucky," said his oldest brother.

*Jimmy war aufgeregt, aber ein bisschen besorgt. „Ich gehe heute nur für zwei Stunden", murmelte er. „Ist das eine lange Zeit?"*

Jimmy was excited but a little bit worried. "I'm only going for two hours today," he murmured. "Is it a long time?"

*„Nicht wirklich", sagte der älteste Bruder. „Du wirst nicht mal bis zum Mittagsschlaf bleiben", fügte der mittlere Bruder hinzu.*

"Not really," said the oldest brother. "You won't even stay for a nap," added the middle brother.

*Während des Frühstücks war Jimmy sehr still. „Bist du bereit zu gehen, Jimmy?", fragte Mama, nachdem er seinen Teller geleert hatte.*

During breakfast Jimmy was very quiet. "Are you ready to go, Jimmy?" Mom asked, after he cleared his plate.

*„Ich denke schon", antwortete er und schaute hinunter auf seinen Teddybären.*

"I guess," he answered looking down at his teddy bear.

*Der Teddybär lächelte ihn groß an und Jimmy fühlte sich viel besser.*

The teddy bear gave him a big smile and Jimmy felt much better.

He took his teddy bear in one hand and Mommy's hand in the other and they set out.



"You'll like it, honey," said Mom while they were walking. "And I'll be back in two hours, right after snack time."



"I know, Mommy. I'm fine. I have my teddy bear with me." Jimmy winked at his bear.



"I'm so proud of you, my big boy," said Mom as the pair walked up to the daycare's door.

*Mama klopfte zweimal an und eine Frau erschien an der Tür.*

Mom knocked twice, and a lady appeared at the door.

*„Hallo, Jimmy", sagte die Frau. „Komm herein! "*
"Hello, Jimmy," the lady said. "Come on in!"

*„Woher kennt sie mich?", flüsterte Jimmy seiner Mama zu.*

"How does she know me?" Jimmy whispered to his mom.

*Mama lächelte. „Ich habe sie vorher angerufen und ihr gesagt, dass wir kommen."*

Mom smiled. "I called her before and told her we were coming."

*Es waren viele andere Kinder dort. Einige von ihnen spielten mit Autos und andere spielten mit Puppen.*

There were a lot of other kids there. Some of them were playing with cars, and others were playing with dolls.

*„Lass uns gehen und Spaß haben. Komm schon, Jimmy!", sagte der Teddybär. Lächelnd drehte sich Jimmy zu Mama um.*

"Let's go have some fun. Come on, Jimmy!" the teddy bear said. Smiling, Jimmy turned to Mom.

*„Geh und hab Spaß, Schatz", sagte sie. „Ich hole dich gleich nach dem Essen ab."*

"Go have fun, sweetie," she said. "I'll pick you up right after snack time."

*„Ich weiß. Tschüss, Mama!", rief Jimmy, als er losrannte, um mit einem großen Truck zu spielen.*

"I remember. Bye, Mom!" Jimmy yelled as he ran to play with a large truck.

After two hours, Mom came back to the daycare to pick up Jimmy. He ran to meet her and gave her a huge hug.



"Mom, it was so much fun!" he shouted. "I played with a large truck, and then I painted a flower for you all by myself!"



Mom smiled happily. "It's so beautiful. What else did you do today?"

*„Die Lehrerin hat uns ein Buch vorgelesen und danach haben wir eine Kleinigkeit gegessen", sagte Jimmy in einem Atemzug und hüpfte neben Mama.*

"The teacher read us a book, and after that we ate a snack," Jimmy said in one breath, bouncing near Mom.

*„Kann ich morgen länger bleiben? Bitte, Mama!"*
"Can I stay for longer tomorrow? Please, Mom!"

*Am nächsten Tag blieb er länger. Am Tag danach blieb er sogar noch länger.*

The next day, he stayed longer. The day after that he stayed even longer.

*Jetzt verbringt Jimmy den ganzen Tag in der Kita und hat viel Spaß! Er spielt gern Spiele und malt gern, er hört gern Geschichten und isst gern.*

Now, Jimmy spends the whole day in daycare having lots of fun! He loves to play games and paint, to hear stories and eat.

*Er freut sich auch, wenn es Zeit ist für den Mittagsschlaf, damit er sich ein wenig ausruhen kann.*

He is also happy when naptime comes, so he can rest a little bit.

*Manchmal nimmt Jimmy den Teddybären nicht mit.*

Sometimes Jimmy doesn't bring teddy bear with him.

*Aber wenn Jimmy aus der Kita nach Hause kommt, erzählt er ihm alles von seinem Tag.*
But when he comes back home from daycare, Jimmy tells him all about his day.